Deep Down Inside

I'll love you forever

ben heller

deep down inside

Copyright 2023 © Ben Heller

All rights reserved. No portion of this book may be reproduced in any form without permission from the publisher, except as permitted by U.S copyright law.

benhellerpoetry@gmail.com

ISBN: 9798858067573
Independently published
Imprint:
Benjamin Pulling
Fistritz 62
3812 Groß-Siegharts

deep down inside

~~for H~~
for 12-year-old me

and *you*, however
old you might be

Author's Note

It's been four years since I published my first ever piece of poetry on Instagram.

Back then, I was writing to heal my heart from heartbreak.

And while I like to think that my heart has healed by now, it was quite a journey.

Deep Down Inside is my attempt to recreate this journey. Starting not at the moment of heartbreak, but from the very beginning:

From falling in love, to being in love, to breaking up, and to eventually falling in love with myself.

Deep Down Inside will let you experience
euphoria, *butterflies*, and *enthusiasm*.
love, *warmth*, and *magic*.
sorrow, *grief*, and *anger*.
harmony, *peace*, and *forgiveness*.

Enjoy the ride.

With love, Ben.

deep down inside

Chapters

1 Finding You

2 Loving You

3 Missing You

4 Finding Myself

deep down inside

1 Finding You

"let go", you whispered, as our secret escape
approached its end.

and I let go of your hand,
just in time,
because the next moment,
I could already spot our friends outside the party
venue.

and so, we came back

as if
nothing ever happened,

as if
we hadn't just broken into the outdoor pool,

as if
we hadn't just kissed for an hour straight.

deep down inside

can we go back to
just friends
if we only
kissed once?

maybe we could.

but can we still go back,
after kissing twice?
sleeping over?
making out?

because I am so damn tired
of losing people,
and I cannot understand
why do we have to cut it off eventually,
once and forever,
never talking to each other again,
never sensing our bond ever again.

only because we kissed each other once?

deep down inside

it was already past midnight, on the way home,
as a sudden wave of tiredness washed over me,
my body feeling heavier and heavier in the
passenger seat,
and as I glanced out the window,
I realized how slowly you were driving

but for some reason,
it was not strange at all,
but made me feel relaxed and comforted.

and as if you could read my thoughts,
you said:
"in case you're wondering why we're driving that
slow – I don't want to run over any deer.
and to be honest – I don't mind spending some more
time with you either"

back then,
those words were the most beautiful thing I had ever
been told.

deep down inside

your hands upon my thighs
don't let me down tonight
just love me like you do
and maybe
only maybe
if it feels alright to you
you might
want to consider
kissing me goodbye
before your hand reaches towards the car door
handle
making way for the cold outside
concluding us
at least for this night

deep down inside

I still remember,
clear and bright,
the smile that followed,
so lightly,
unforced,
so natural and true,
as I made way for home
with your silhouette still in the rearview mirror,
wondering,
am I really going home

or did home just leave with you?

deep down inside

but can home be a person?

and if so,
should home be a person?

or is it naive
to assign this powerful word to a human being?

and if it is naive,
what kind of naive it might be?
a beautiful one?
a hopeless romantic one?
or just a stupid one?

for tonight I will not care

as I got nowhere else to go

deep down inside

the truth is,
I never liked going out,
I never enjoyed meeting the same boring people at
the same boring parties weekend for weekend,
and I especially always hated the days after

the truth is: you.

you are the reason I wasted my youth like that,
attending the same boring parties weekend for
weekend,
because nowhere else did I have a higher chance of
running into you,
let alone kissing you.

and that one thing – your lips against mine – was
what I desired the most.
and so, I did what I did.

deep down inside

there's something about you magically attracting me,
and I can't name what it is,
cause else it wouldn't be magic I suppose?

but sometimes,
when I lay awake at night,
my little brain wants to decipher what my heart
won't tell.

then I start to think:
maybe it's the way you wrap the taxi driver round
your finger,
maybe it's the way even the largest of all much too
large rain ponchos looks stunning when you dance in
it at the festival,
or maybe it's the way I become one with the
universe every time our fingers intertwine

deep down inside

summer 2019
party outdoors
late at night
blurry memory log - wouldn't bet too much on it.

we had finished high school,
predrinks at my best friend's,
speakers on maximum volume,
in the moment we were infinite.

time to go.
I take the right back seat,
leaning out of the window,
warm wind blows through our hair,

only two more minutes left to drive,
I pray silently you'd be there.
leave some money at the entrance
start to look if you're around.

and as if you had been waiting,
our eyes meet under the disco lights,
and as if you had been praying for me to be there too,
our lips meet under the midnight star sky.

deep down inside

and suddenly,
all the world went quiet

and suddenly,
all the fear disappeared

and suddenly,
all the dark was lit up

because suddenly,
I stumbled into you

deep down inside

I never look for love,
but when love finds me,
I agreed with myself to fully embrace it

because if something I was never looking for finds me,
how could I not put my trust in the universe?

deep down inside

first encounter awkwardness,
first-hour retention,
second hour tension build up,
first movie cuddles,

oh, how I hate it and I love it at the same time

deep down inside

I don't want to kiss you goodbye today
how about we just hug each other instead?

though just does not fit here,
because a hug is not just a hug

it is your body against mine,
our souls' materializations colliding,
a language of love
too often not done justice

people kiss all the time
on first dates,
though there won't be a second one,
drunk at parties,
though they won't remember each other's names in the morning

that's why I prefer movies
that end not with a kiss
but a genuine and unforced hug
far from any ulterior motives

so how about we just hug each other this time?

deep down inside

I am not asking you for anything
but a forever-lasting honesty,
because honestly,
I am so tired of being lied to,
so do not let me suffer

for allowing myself to like you

deep down inside

trust is a dangerous thing
making you vulnerable
taking you inner peace
and carrying it to the last possible bit of
a cliff so steep
it hurts to look down

but what would we be without trust
without connection, love, and lust?

so take that hurt and fear
breath it in
embrace it

because even if you fall
there'll be deep blue water somewhere far down
hard as steel at first
but softer over time

you know it deep down inside

deep down inside

scared to jump, she jumped
with peace to lose and joy to gain.

the sight of a genuine connection,
even if far out on the misty horizon
made her forget the devils of her past,
the trauma and the scars

deep down inside

what if
I hadn't said "yes" to going out despite being way too tired?

what if
you hadn't run into me despite there being 1,000 other people in the club?

then
we wouldn't have ruined our friendship by kissing for 2 hours straight.

deep down inside

I don't believe in magic,
yet when we are together,
you seem to make time stand still,
but then,
before I notice,
hours have passed
that felt like minutes at most,

I don't believe in magic
and I never really liked physics at school,
but there's this one thing I remember:
that time is relative and
that time can be bent,
and maybe that's what you do

or could it be that I'm in love with you?

deep down inside

»or could it be that
I'm in love with you?«

deep down inside

2 Loving You

I had nothing to lose and nowhere to go,
yet I went,
step by step I kept moving on,
not knowing where I was heading,

and then I stumbled into you,
and realized,
everything happens for a reason,
and it was you for whom I took that first step

deep down inside

the moment I met you,
a tiny little wave was born in the ocean deep down inside of me

and with every word you said,
and every action you took,
that wave became bigger

until it had grown so big,
lurking at the edge of my heart,
that it was waiting for nothing more than one final tiny spark

and then it hit me,
everything, all at once

your lips were the spark,
and the wave broke over me

deep down inside

I fell in love with you
and the way you love this world.

I fell in love with your smile
and the happiness it brings to the world.

I fell in love with your warmth
and how it comforts those close to you.

And I fell in love with your sadness and tears,
which the world always soaks up for you.

deep down inside

enjoy the butterflies,

enjoy the first kiss after
a long night of dancing
to your favorite teenage songs,

enjoy the first sleepover
though you have to get up
early the next morning,

enjoy the love.

deep down inside

it was already past midnight,
on our way home from the theater,
as a severe thunderstorm suddenly rolled in on us,
but luckily,
you had brought an umbrella with you,
and when you opened it to protect us from the heavy rain,
in that very moment right there,
you had created another world for us,
and while we had no more than this tiny space under the umbrella,
sharing it with you that night made it beyond magical

deep down inside

'right person, right time' was never more than a science
fiction utopia for me,
or at least so I thought,
because when I met you, I realized,
this stuff actually happens

deep down inside

I was never really looking for you,
yet I found you.

at an unexpected time,
at an unexpected place,
an unexpected, extraordinary person entered my life

and it wasn't for long until you became part of my life

the late-night calls,
the morning messages,
the weekend commutes,
the hours on the train,
the lightness of being together,
the melancholy of leaving on a Sunday

crossing borders,
extending reality

I am beyond grateful that we met

deep down inside

loving you feels like

the first night in a foreign city,
the last day of school,
the first snow of the year on a cozy winter's morning,
the last sunrays by the beach

deep down inside

you add a hell lot of lightness to my life,
because

whatever happens,
wherever I take the wrong turn,
and whenever I fall,

I will never fall deeper and harder than into your soft arms

deep down inside

you and the sea,

you are

beautiful

sparkling

serenely smooth from afar

mysterious underneath the surface

keeper of unforeseeable secrets in your depths.

sometimes you're calm and inviting,

warm and embracing,

sometimes you're rough and forbidding, cold and swallowing.

you are magical, mesmerizing, breathtaking,

addictive,

my yearning for you starts the second we depart.

deep down inside

I want to sit down with you in the warm sand on an Atlantic beach at sunset,
I want to take your hand,
I want to lay my head on your shoulder,
I want to watch the sun go down and the moon rise,
I want to have the deepest conversation with you all night,
I want to gaze at the stars with you,
and at the sight of the first shooting star,
I'll make a wish,
that we'll love each other until the end of times

deep down inside

in this world of infinite opportunities,
we can be anything, not everything,
and while I don't know exactly yet
what
where
and who
I want to be,
I know for certain that
it is you I want to be with.

deep down inside

I don't want 'us against the world',
I want 'us with the world',
because why fight something
that holds so much beauty for us to explore

so many conversations to follow,
so many places to discover,
so many flavors to taste,
so many songs to listen to,
so much art to get lost in.

and when the days end,
we'll still be together, and we'll talk about all those things,
about the good and the bad,
and how nothing ever even got close to tearing us apart,
as it has always been 'us with the world'.

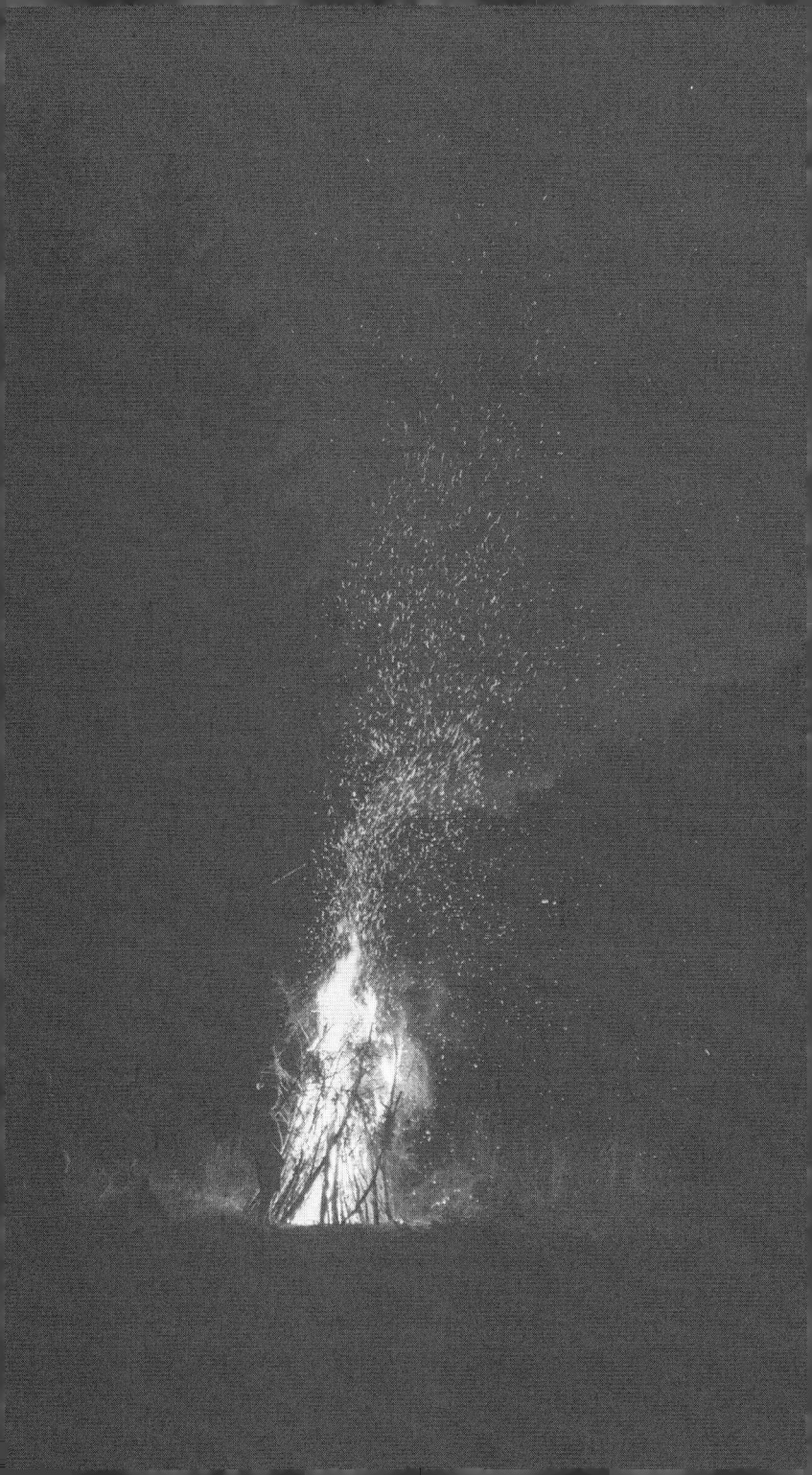

deep down inside

they always say that
you cannot be loved by anyone
if you do not love yourself,

and that
you cannot be happy with someone else
if you're unhappy on your own,

but I was not happy,
and God,
I did not love myself

but I met you
and you did not care what they say

you found me at my worst,
held me together when I wanted to fall apart,
and gave me so much hope when you said

'we'll make it work together'

deep down inside

loving you feels like

a cup of hot tea on a snowy winter's day,
heavy rain against the windows,
forgotten songs rediscovered,
the view from the top after a morning hike

deep down inside

my favorite place in the world?
your arms.

my favorite sound in the world?
your laugh.

my favorite taste in the world?
your lips.

my favorite person in the world?
you, you, only you.

deep down inside

I don't need you,

you don't need me,

and yet we want each other so so much

and I think that's the best about us

deep down inside

»tell me, when do you feel most alive?«
»with you I feel most alive«

with you I come alive because
you know me the way I really am,
with you I am myself,
with you I feel safe,
with you, any place is my happy place

deep down inside

I love you,
because

I lose the sense of time when we talk late at night,
I lose all self-doubts when you tell me I'm fine
I lose all fears when I lie in your arms,

and with all those things lost, our love's the greatest
win

deep down inside

I find myself in a windy night,
with pouring rain outside,
cuddled up in bed with you,
with only the cloudy skylight above your bed
shielding us from the rain and cold.
you have fallen asleep in my arms, I realize,
so, I won't make a move to not wake you,
instead, I watch the raindrops patter against the glass,
which appears fragile and breakable, yet steadfastly shields us.
I listen to your heartbeat and breath,
which is slow and peaceful right now,
and draw the connection between the window and our hearts: they're fragile and could break at any time.
yet we entrust our hearts to one another,
because despite knowing the risk,
it is so worth it loving you.

the thought overwhelms me, causing me to hold you a tiny bit too tight,
so you wake up to kiss me goodnight.

deep down inside

Sometimes I hate myself for all this overthinking,
because there's times when I just can't focus on the moment,
no matter how much I want it,
no matter how hard I try.
And the harder I try, the more distant I become.
One moment, I am holding you under a night sky
full of starts in the outside area of our favorite
thermal bath, at peace with you, us, myself, bonded
with you and the universe.
but already in the next moment, I picture myself
messing it all up,
and then suddenly after that,
the thoughts rapidly enter my mind, urging me to
question it all,
giving me anxiety,
and a guilty conscience for no reason,
wondering what would be if I weren't with you,
and I hate those thoughts and I don't want them,
but no matter how hard I try,
I just can't stop overthinking.

deep down inside

If you want to go,

then go,

but please do it subtle, slow, and soft,

and don't run,

because

I don't want to feel like I'm someone to run from,

and the last person I would want that to do is you.

Be gentle with me,

even as you're leaving,

and remember,

why you once settled.

please,

do me this one last favor.

deep down inside

»I don't want to feel like I am someone to run from.«

deep down inside

3 Missing You

my world was falling apart,

on the day I had to learn,

the greatest pain there is,

is not caused by someone

but someone's absence

deep down inside

for all my life
I have always known when it was time to go
to leave and to move on

there's moments to share
but then at one distinct point in time
this moment arrives
when there is nothing left to say
nothing left to do but go

when it's time for
turning to myself,
talking to myself,
crying on my own,
processing thoughts and feelings and memories by
myself

maybe calling my friends
introducing them on the matter,
but in this very moment with you
I decided to turn against my own principles

so I stayed,
standing in the door frame of your room,
looking back one final time,
asking you

can I stay just one more night?

deep down inside

Did you get home okay?

I did,
I tell you
crying in my bed

I did,
I tell you,
after waiting for two hours in the soaring rain
right where you left me

eventually calling my mum
cause I got no one else to pick me up

crying in the car on the drive home

but yeah

I guess I did get home okay

deep down inside

7 am
I turn off the alarm and make way for the bathroom
I take a quick shower,
throw on some clothes
and head to the kitchen
where I make coffee for two.
two?
why two?
the two of us.
us?
why us?
didn't we break up the night before in a gruesome
fight?
we did,
my mind reminds me,
as the memories of last night felt more like a bad
dream than reality,
but they are reality now,
that's for sure.
and I must accept that reality if I want to ever move
on.
I want,
I say to myself,
before I take your cup of coffee and pour it down the
sink

deep down inside

infinity
or 412 days?

forever
or until you get bored with me?

always
or until you find someone "better"?

deep down inside

I don't want to go get my things,
pick them up from your room,
where everything carries your scent.
I don't want to text you 'I'm here',
without any emojis,
cause we're serious and cold now.
I don't want to wait for you to open up your door,
letting me in,
into something we once shared,
but now is no longer a space I should be at.
I don't want to say 'yes',
when you offer me a glass of water,
just so that we can delay the most final of all
goodbyes for two damn minutes.

I don't want to be in your room,
because you know what?
that vintage sweater that's still in there,
the one I continuously referred to as 'my favorite one'

is no longer my favorite one,
and I don't want it anymore

maybe I'll miss it

I don't know
but I know one thing for sure

I'll miss you more

deep down inside

Isn't it strange how you're driving me insane,
but at the same time,
you're the one to numb the pain?

deep down inside

there's a million different stories about lovers who
are hurt

maybe cancer,
maybe wars,
or cause titanic had to burst

out of all these different stories,
ours is the worst

I wonder what you're gonna tell them?

oh, she just didn't text me first?

deep down inside

you left,
I'm hearbroken,

so, now there's 2 options how to proceed:

option 1 is what I call the super-unrealistic-and-very-likely-insanely-unhealthy-for-my-own-mental-health-option: waiting for you to come back to me

option 2 is what I call the super-hurtful-yet-likely-better-for-myself-option: trying to forget you

to be honest,
I don't know what to do,
I kinda want to pursue both options and none at the same time.

deep down inside

when I first met you,
I got to discover a whole new world,
and I was stupid enough to get fully ingaged in that
world and to leave my old one behind,
because when I last met you,
you destroyed both of those worlds,
the one you brought with you,
and the one I abandoned for you.

my new world?
it is dark, cold, empty and grey.
there isn't much to do here,
so I cry, hope and pray,
that one day I will restore my own world to its
former beauty,
which once finished,
I will never let go off for someone else,
never ever again.

deep down inside

it took my 3 seconds
to fall in love with you.

it took me 3 years
to get over you.

and it will take me an eternity
to forget you.

deep down inside

if only for a moment I could still
lay my head on your shoulder,

then you could stop my darkest nights
from getting colder,

but we both now
we do not work out when sober.

deep down inside

it will never be the same again,

and we will never be the same again,

I just hope there's a way for us to be together again,

some way or another,

even if it won't be the same again

deep down inside

it made me think of you

'what made you think of me?'

the songs on the radio,
the pictures on the wall,
the couple in the coffee,
the empty space in my bed,
your hoodie in my closet,

everything in this world makes me think of you.

deep down inside

our shared memories are so vivid within me.

every laughter,

& every fight

I can't stop thinking about you.

every day,

& every night

deep down inside

you wanted to take me Paris
remember?
I was yours
& you were mine
and that one summer night we swore we would
cherish,
every moment we shared with each other,
all the hugs, kisses, joy, and the laughter,
and I did but I'm starting to doubt,
did you do it too cause I'm crying here without you,
cause you're not there for me anymore

deep down inside

this part of my life is called:

wanting you back so much I started digging out all of our old memories,

scrolling through years old WhatsApp chats until I cry myself to sleep,

regretting all the words I said and the ones I should have told you instead

deep down inside

Sunday mornings are the hardest
when the dopamine from the night out before is
gone,
and my heart is longing for you to hold me so
heavily that it feels as if it might burst
into thousand tiny pieces,
I miss you,
and I kind of want to tell you,
but I know it wouldn't change anything,
so I don't

deep down inside

last night you were in my dreams,
looked me in the eye,
god
it felt so real

it was as if you were here again,
deep down inside me feel

and when the light came to wake me,
and you slowly starting to fade away,
my soul was longing for you to take me,
but instead,
I must live without you
for another day

deep down inside

there's others out there as well
yeah sure but I don't want them
there's more for you to see
people will love you who you haven't even met yet

but what if I don't want them
cause all I want is you?

deep down inside

I gave you everything I could,
yet my everything was never enough for you.

& I loved you with all my heart,
yet my love was never enough for you.

deep down inside

if they ask me how I fell
I will always say alright
cause I've learnt how to keep
all my tears for the night

deep down inside

when I met you,
it was the right person, wrong time

but how can I know
that the right time will still come in this life?

deep down inside

I don't want to hear you apologize,
I want the old you back with me here in this bed tonight,
a version of you that never existed outside of my head,
a version of you that would never have said what you said

a version of you that would never leave me so damn sad,
a version of you without twenty thousand flags in pure red,
a version of you that would have stayed for the darkest nights,
a version of you whose wrongs would not have destroyed all our rights

deep down inside

I don't miss you,
no,
definitely not,
I most definitely never think about you,
I don't think about how we first met,
I don't think about that look you gave me,
I don't think about how we first kissed in the pouring rain,
I don't think about when you first slept over,
I don't think about how you first said 'I love you' early in the morning with that cute sleepy voice of yours,
oh,
maybe I do still think about you

deep down inside

I tell my friends I don't
miss you anymore,
yet I think about you
all the time.

I tell my mum we weren't
really together anyways,
yet we used to daydream
about marriage and kids.

I tell my mind I never
really loved you anyways,
yet my heart yearns for
you to come back.

deep down inside

it's been years since we last talked,
yet when I see you with your new love,
I see a picture of 18-year-old us
making out in the rain

it's been years since we last talked,
yet when I accidentally open up our chat,
I see a picture of 17-year-old me
staring at your messages with the biggest smile

deep down inside

do you still think about me when my name drops at the party?

do you still go through our pictures,
or do they rest in 'last deleted',
waiting to be gone once and for all?

do you sometimes think about how our lives would have gone differently?

what if we never split up?

deep down inside

maybe I wanted you so much
that my brain was like
"we usually want what we can't have"

and so, my mind shifted from thoughts of "I want you" to "I can't have you"

and guess what happened?
guess where I stand 4 years later?

I still want you and I still can't have you

deep down inside

I grew increasingly nervous as I moved closer to the club entrance,
when the bouncer suddenly called for me,
"come, we have a special place for you here", he said.
it was then, that it struck me – I had no idea where I was,
"what is this place?", I asked.
"this, dear friend, is the broken hearts club. you're safe and more than welcome here."
next, I was overwhelmed by a torrent of painful memories – of the night you confessed your sickening lies to me; of the day I collected all my belongings from your place, tears streaming down my face; of …

…

I decide it's time to stop thinking about it.

I decide to lay the past to rest.

I decide to step into this place.

I decide to enter the broken hearts club.

deep down inside

»I decide to
lay the past to rest.«

4 Finding Myself

I was so madly in love with you,
I couldn't get myself out of bed the days after
spending the night with you,
I'd get mad with my mum for no reason just because
you depleted all my dopamine,
because without you, the world seemed so empty,
gray, and boring.

but as time passes,
it becomes clearer and clearer,
that you never really loved me back,
and that I was never more than a convenience to you,
and it breaks me, and I feel bad for letting you empty
my world back then.

deep down inside

if »I love you« was a lie,
if »I want you« was for no more than one night,

then how could you hold me so tight?
how could you pretend we'd be forever together &
everything'd be alright?

deep down inside

I still feel guilty to this day

for allowing myself to feel a glimmer of relief

when my friends passed me the message

that after I kissed that other boy at the party,

you had been crying throughout the whole drive home.

Maybe this makes me a bad person,

I don't know,

but it paved the way for me

to finally believe

that you did care about me, at least a little bit.

deep down inside

I mistook endorphins
for happiness,
I mistook butterflies
for tenderness,
I mistook late-night calls
for genuine affection,
but in the end, I was nothing
more to you

than a temporary distraction

deep down inside

I think you never really liked me
I think you only ever liked the feeling of me wanting you,
and the more I think about it,
the more it breaks me

deep down inside

I was crazy enough
to believe I could change you,

I was stupid enough
to believe you truly cared about me,

I was naive enough
to ignore all your red flags flying high,

and I was too anxious
to end us when I finally saw them.

deep down inside

you kept asking for more
while I already gave you all I had

deep down inside

the truth is
I never loved you

I only ever loved a
version of you that
never existed outside
of my thoughts

deep down inside

when did you fall out of love with me?

because I had not seen it coming,
my world falling apart the moment you told me

but looking back,
I start to remember more and more situations in
which you kind of made it obvious.

maybe I did not want to see it,
because I was blindly in love.

deep down inside

at first,
I was heartbroken because of you
and trust me,
that heartbreak was devastating

the days after,
I did not leave my bed,
all I did was crying
& being sad

but then something unusual and unexpected happen,
which is hard to describe but anyways, here's my
take on it:

I think I was so madly admiring you, that after
falling in love with you and after you have taken
away from me the possibility of being in love with
you,
I was slowly falling in love with being heartbroken
because of you

because I was thinking that if I can't be with you,
then better having my heart broken by you than
having nothing to do with you

deep down inside

what if

the two of us had never met

what if

the two of us had never kissed

what if

the two of us had never fallen in love

because sometimes I wonder,

would I not miss you had we never met?

deep down inside

we were everything we ever wanted,
everything we ever needed.

we were such a ridiculously perfect match,
it felt as if we had conquered the world by simply
lying in each other's arms.

and that's exactly what we did,
perhaps a little too often, perhaps a little too long
until the cries of the world became too loud for us to
ignore,
whispering 'this isn't everything, this is not the end'

and so we split up,
because the world needed us more than we needed
each other.

deep down inside

I still think about you,
sometimes a lot,
and sometimes more than a lot

and I wonder if you still think about me,
if I am still there somewhere in your thoughts,
or if I have become a forgotten page in your story,
which has come to an end last summer

perhaps too soon,
perhaps too abrupt,
and perhaps too unexpected

but for now, I am okay with that,
because some people are meant to last only for a phase

deep down inside

this is not the end of the world,
even if it feels like that

the sun will rise again,
rain will fall again,
lightning will strike again,
thunder will roll again,
the birds will sing once more,
there'll be love waiting outside your door,
a world to explore,
beauty to be found,
memories to be made

this is not the end of the world

only the end of us

deep down inside

I'll do my best to remember the happy moments of
our story,
they'll always hold a special place in my heart,
but I also acknowledge that right beside those
memories, my heart now has a breaking point

deep down inside

'never go to sleep angry. because what if …'

that's what they always say

and I believe that's a good value to live by,
but for all my life I confused the above with settling disputes

and only now have I come to realize that's not quite true.
because if the other person does not want to settle
the dispute & does not want to forgive you,
forgiving them is all you can do.

everything else is not within your power,
and that's okay

so, forgive and go get your sleep.
you deserve it.

deep down inside

breaking up is a choice about the future,
not the past

so do not let it devalue your together memories

because we can only ever fall out of love,
if we have fallen in love with each other before

deep down inside

if you ever fall in love again
I hope he'll love you better than I did,
and that he won't ever break your heart,
neither the way I broke it nor any other way,
because who am I to wish you harm?

if you ever choose to let someone get so close to you again,
I hope it will be a choice you won't regret again,
and given that,
I hope this someone new will get even closer than I had ever gotten (it hurts so bad to say this, but I genuinely wish you'll be happier than you were with me)

deep down inside

I hope you still think about me,
but not in an obsessive way

I don't want you to miss me,
crying alone in your bed

I want you to live your life to the fullest,
even if I am no longer part of your present life

but I was part of your past life,
and I hope I am still deep down there,
somewhere in your favorite memories

I want you to move on,
yet never forget me

deep down inside

he was not the one for you.

you might not see that now,
you might not believe me today
and probably won't do so tomorrow,

but eventually,
and if it takes 10 years,
you will see it too

he was not the one for you

deep down inside

memories in the rear-view mirror may appear closer
than they are

so
let
those
moments
rest

throw
that
hoodie
out

clear
that
'last deleted'
folder

and focus on the future.

you deserve it

deep down inside

if I were given a certain contingent of days that I could spend with you,
I would have reserved those days for a later stage in my life,
in which the battle with myself has hopefully come to an end,
when I would be capable of giving you the love you deserve

deep down inside

I don't remember what you look like,
I lost the memory of how you smell,
I have no idea what you're up to,
but I miss the sound of your laugh

it's been a long time since we last spoke,
it's been a lot longer since we last loved,
and I don't know if we will ever meet again,
in any case, I sincerely wish you a life as sweet as cinnamon.

deep down inside

one day you'll forget him,

one day you'll be happy again,

and one day you'll be happier than ever before,

one

day

it will all make sense <3

deep down inside

deep down inside

you will always have a place in my heart,

no matter where you are,

no matter where you go,

no matter who you'll kiss,

no matter who you'll hold,

no matter whose shirts you'll wear,

this tiny place inside my heart remains reserved for

you, remains filled with your love,

and the warmth,

and the sparks,

I felt in summer 18

when the two of us still used to be

naive teenagers with slightly too big dreams

deep down inside

I don't want you back,
but sometimes, I fall down this deep black hole of recalling memories
from a time long ago where we'd share the same bus to the same high school,
attend the same parties on the weekends,
where I'd be waiting nervously at the front door for you to pick me up in your mum's car,
where I'd wear my best dresses to go nowhere in particular,
and where it didn't even matter because I was with you,
adrenaline and dopamine rushing through my veins,
my heart beating fast,
my hair in the wind,
I felt so nervous and happy back then.
I'm so glad we used to have it all,
oh maybe I should take the courage to type your number and press 'call'.

deep down inside

for all my life I was comparing myself
with others,
for all my life I felt miserable,
but then I realized this one thing:

I am neither worse than others nor should I strive for being better than others,

because *I* am *myself*

& in the end,

no one could *ever* be better at *being myself* than I can

deep down inside

I wish you nothing but joy and good times
even if I won't be the one to share it with

I wish you no harm
even if I won't be the one you'd call
when life gets dark
and you need a soul to hold on to,
a shoulder to cry,
or a hand to hold

I encourage you to grow
even if I won't be the one to foster that growth,
to whisper words of courage

because after all
we are still on the same team
even if we play different games now,
walk different paths,
and make memories on our own

because maybe one day
our paths will cross again
and our souls will intertwine
once more and forever

and even if not
who am I to wish you harm?

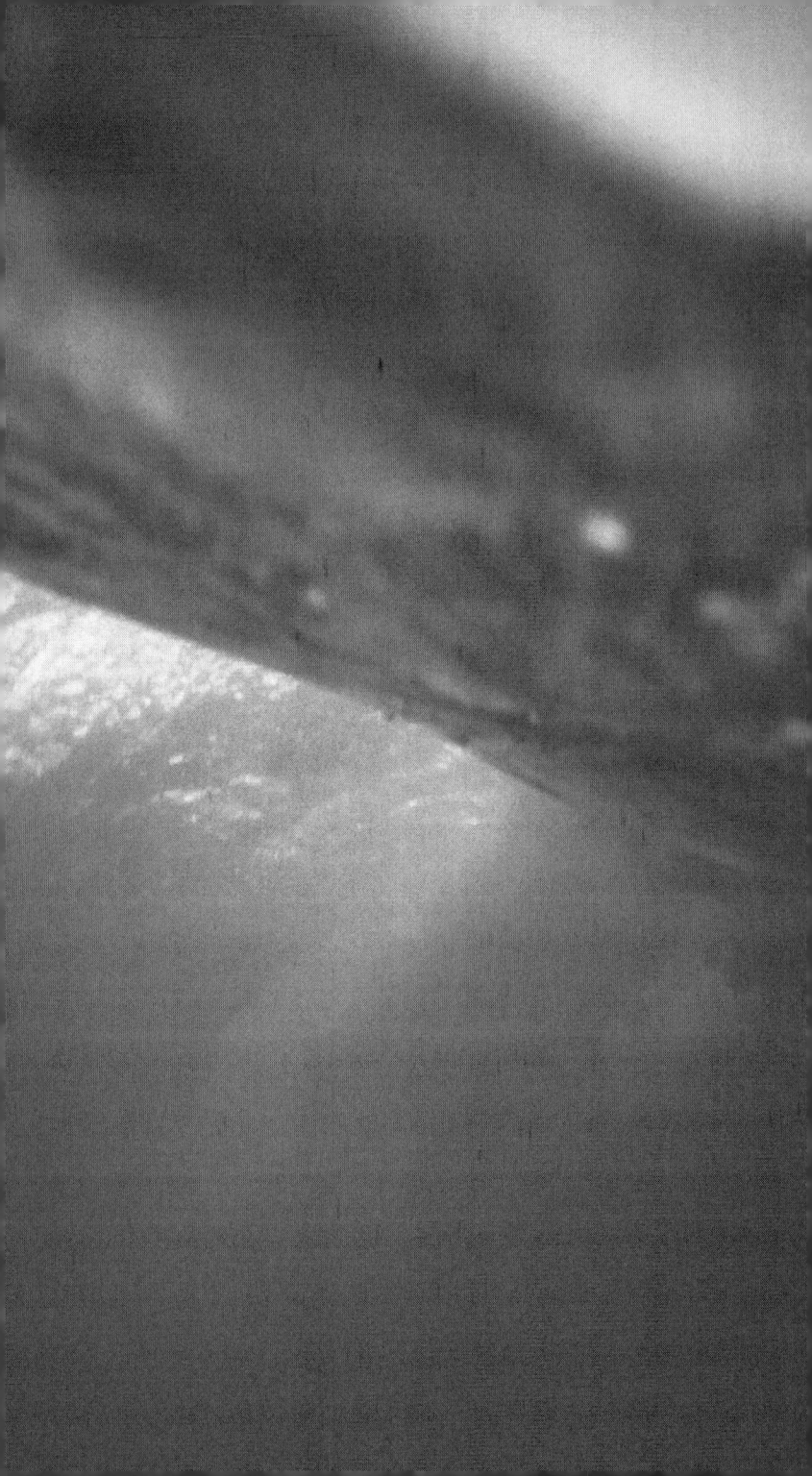

deep down inside

»who am I to wish you harm?«

deep down inside

getting to know you was unexpected,
magical
and many first times at once.

falling in love with you was easy,
effortless,
and beautiful.

falling out of love was hard,
challenging,
and incredibly ugly.

but then **I fell in love with myself**,
and falling in love with myself has healed
all the scars of my past.

Epilogue

Thank you for giving these words a home with you.

And no matter the journey you are on, always remember that I am with you.

Making this book took me countless sleepless nights (and more nerves than I thought I had).

So if you enjoyed reading – which I hope from the bottom of my heart – please consider leaving me a review on Amazon – (so that others can find this book as well).

If you want to reach out to me, you can do so via email (benhellerpoetry@gmail.com) or TikTok (benhellerpoetry).

With love, Ben

Printed in Great Britain
by Amazon